What Others Are Saying

THE MIDWEST BOOK REVIEW

"Every novel, regardless of its genre, needs to open with a hook, and then irresistibly propel the reader to dive in and become immersed in the story from beginning to end. ROBIN by Kenneth Shelby Armstrong is just such a novel and highly recommended as an original and carefully crafted story from first page to last."

James A. Cox, Editor-in-Chief

Marilyn A. Hudson
Armstrong's "Robin" Soars High.

"Oklahoma author Kenneth Shelby Armstrong presents a story of lyrical beauty, deeply felt emotion, thought provoking actions, and lasting inspiration."

Marilyn A. Hudson Reviewer

"An interesting, even compelling collection. Some of the essays have phrases that have that lasting impact worth repeating, rising to the level of superb writing."

T. W. Jones, attorney at Law
Colorado Springs, Colorado

"Armstrong shows unusual insight into his subject and has the literary skill to express it forcefully and meaningfully."

Val J. Christensen, Ph.D.
Educator, San Diego, California

"I read your book in one sitting. It is truly a fine piece of work. . . Your writing is superb."
                      James D. Hamilton, Ed.D.
                      Psychologist,
                      Austin, Colorado

"Great project! I've never seen a similar one."
                      Forrest Ladd, Ph.D.
                      University Vice President
                      Bethany, Oklahoma

"I have your book in hand. Oh, what a choice of words. A literary masterpiece straight from the heart."
                      Sam Stearman,
                      Co-founder ARMM

"The wit, wisdom and wealth of words that powerfully communicate from your soul to ours, is a gift and anointing I've known of you for 55 years. Keep it up."
                      Walter Thomas, Ed.D.
                      Educator, Speaker, Motivater

"Fascinating experience, and one that I did not know you had! Indeed your life seems to unfold into a story book of rich adventures, each a puzzle piece in a most dynamic, influential and inspirational life!"
                      Vivian Stewart
                      Poet, Author, Artist, Creator

Win With WisdomSeries

Kenneth Shelby Armstrong Th.D., Ed.D.

Copyright © 2017

ALL RIGHTS RESERVED.
NO PART OF THIS BOOK MAY BE REPRODUCED
OR TRANSMITTED IN ANY FORM OR BY ANY MEANS,
ELECTRONIC OR MECHANICAL, INCLUDING
PHOTOCOPYING, RECORDING OR
BY ANY INFORMATION STORAGE AND RETRIEVAL
SYSTEM, WITHOUT WRITTEN PERMISSION FROM THE
AUTHOR.

The Series

Introduction

I entered the digital age in the early 1980s. I did not expect to enter at such a digital time, but it was thrust upon me when they placed a brand new Macintosh computer on my desk. It was a strange looking box. I found that it had a keyboard just like my old typewriter, and added to that was a screen just like my small television set at home. The digital age had found me. It was a brand new age—complex but malleable.

It was not long until the *internet* was available, and hardly knowing what I was facing, I lurched onward and upward—exploring a whole new universe of learning. Email arrived early and demanded attention which strained the learning curve again. Wonderful new programs brought excitement and possibilities never before dreamed of. This series of books was the product of many hours of study and learning.

There are six books in this series. Each has at its core the concept of wisdom. And as you will shortly see, this concept is valuable to the individual, the institution, and the nation. Yes, the nation—America—has its own peculiar wisdom and that wisdom has been displayed in its wars, economics, and ethos.

Our focus in this chapter, however is the kind of wisdom that is useful to the individual. Of primary importance is "**how you can get things done.**"

Wise Methods for Wise People

Ten Steps to Reaching Your Goals.

We do a lot of things in life, but we seldom stop to ask "How did I learn to do this—*this* way?" Perhaps the person who taught me how to do things this way did not know herself how this process should have been done. Often, without thinking, we continue doing the process the same way someone first taught us.

Each morning we start the same routine. We put on our under-clothes, then we put both of our socks on—then our shoes. We never waiver in the process. Perhaps, however, we should put just one sock on, and then the shoe. Next we put the other sock on, and then the other shoe. In all probability we start with the left foot first and then the right foot. And, if for some reason we put the sock on the right foot first, we don't feel quite right. We started wrong, and what else will be wrong during our day?

The point i that much of what we do each day has been predetermined by much earlier lessons on how to do particular things. What if we were taught wrong? What if there are much better ways of doing things, and we don't know about them?

I think it was Descartes who came to the realization that he had all of these ideas in his head and he didn't know who put them in there. Finally, he determined to bring each item out and examine it. After examining an item he could either toss it out or invite it back in. Then he knew that whatever was in his head was in there for a reason. He had examined it and invited it in.

Few of us ever go to that trouble. If it is in our heads, we act on it—valid or not—good or bad. It is just too much effort to examine everything that we believe or think, so we just take the easy paths through life, and let others continue to stuff our heads with nonsense. And, of course we do our own part in filling our minds with junk ideas and impossible schemes.

Sometimes we get a great idea that seems so powerful that we immediately adopt it for development. More often than not, months later the luster is gone, and we are disappointed, and all of the people that we have involved in the project have lost their enthusiasm.

Of course, all the money and time is gone, and will never be reclaimed. And the volunteers will not be so willing to consider a new idea in the future. At that point we have started that long walk through the wide end of the tunnel of dreams, but soon we will be looking at a very small hole at the other end. We seldom squeeze through.

In doing research for this book I came across two names that led all the rest. David Allen, a New York Times best selling author, wrote <u>Getting Things Done, the art of stress-free productivity.</u>

This book seemed to be the leader in the field of GTD (Getting Things Done), so I read the 317 pages of advice. It was a great read, but after I had finished it several hours and days later, I asked myself "how many of the people that I work with would actually read the entire volume."

I could tell that the book was well written and that the author was probably a graduate of one of the ivy-league schools. I concluded that he had not recently talked with a barely-educated high school person. He had tapped into the executive market of the top 500 corporations, and he was amply rewarded for that relationship. On the other hand, my interest is in helping the average person learn how to GTD.

The second name prominent in the field was Peter Drucker, author of *The Effective Executive: The Definitive Guide too Getting the Right Things Done*. I had read other books written by Peter Drucker, and this once again was not disappointment. I could tell that he was also an ivy-league product.

I read the 178 pages and felt that it was profitable to me, but would not be avidly read by average people. The CEO of IBM would love it and would probably recommend it to members of his staff. Candidly, I believe that most of his personnel would find themselves too busy to read it on their own time.

Both books were written from the viewpoint of an executive of a large business enterprise and for the benefit of a significant executive. Contrarily, the need for help is from the average businessperson who has never been to Boston, and scarcely aware of what the initials I.B.M. stand for.

This small book is written for the owner of an auto supply store in Round Rock, Texas or the assistant manager of the local Walmart store. (And, possibly the president of Safeway Stores could learn something from reading this book. It would only take him about an hour of time and only $6.00 of cold cash.).

All that being said, I commend you to learning these Ten Steps, and thinking how you can use them to bring success to your door.

**Step One
What Is The Objective?**

Determining that you have at least one important objective in any venture is a good start, but soon you will find out that making that determination is not as easy as it might appear. You will find that your objective may have all sorts of short term ramifications and long term ramifications. It is imperative that these distinctions be made and understood before you go any farther.

I discovered early in my professional life that objectives are obstreperous. They will move and morph in unusual ways. If you do not keep your eyes on them, one day you will notice that they have evolved into a form totally inconsistent with their birth.

It might be wise to have someone tattoo your objective on your forehead, so that every time you look in a mirror, you will see its unwavering form again. Chisel it in granite and carry it with you. Don't let it get out of your sight even for a minute, for it is the one thing that will keep you on course even when there are a dozen reasons to change it.

Objectives will be challenged. And the challenges are good and valuable. Don't avoid the challenges, for they can bolster your objectives. Days, weeks, months, years later you can thank the challengers for helping you build something valuable and useful. Without them you will find that you have a 300 pound baby—still in diapers.

Let me illustrate.

I found myself the president of a small college that had an administrative staff of energetic, bright, and young "movers and shakers." They were sometimes a dream team, but sometimes they were a nightmare. They were as wiggely as a can of worms and on any particular day could be captured with wild out-of-the-world concepts.

Some were good and some were bad. Of particular note in the administration was a young academic professor, brilliant. energetic. Nearly every time that he went to some academic convention, he would return enthused and excited. His first words would usually be, "You know what we ought to do?" And then he would pour forth a great idea that he had conceived or copied while he was gone. His grand idea was usually precipitated by some convention speaker that he had heard. And, he was always convinced that time was of the essence and that we should immediately start the wheels rolling in that direction.

He was so excited about the possibility, that I found myself caught up in his enthusiasm, and I turned my attention to ways that we could make it happen. A few days later I would bring up the subject to him, only to find that the fire had gone out, and he had found something new that we should consider.

But, he was not the only one with that tendency. I discovered that others went through the same process. I was amazed to learn that many bright young people had experienced the process of discovering a pearl of great price, but had not learned how to wrestle it from the clam that was 100 feet below the turbulent sea. Was there any hope?

As I think about it, I was young too, and I had not yet created a useful method for getting things done. It took years for our team to develop a schema for guiding a person through the process of successfully reaching a desired goal. We learned that the first thing in the process is always to know and establish a clear objective for each venture. Cling to it. Never let it go. It is the reason for everything that you do.

**Step Two
What Program Will Help Us
Reach Our Objective?**

Programs should never precede *objectives*. This is one of the most common mistakes that people make. They see a good program and want to institute it immediately. They seldom stop to ask whether it was created to reach a particular important objective or not. Many programs take you no place. They require a lot of time and money, but when they are completed you are **nowhere**.

Most books take you **nowhere**. When you finish the last page, you have no place to go. Many sermons take you no place. You often hear them and then you comment, "That was nice." But it took you **nowhere**.

Teachers are avid about developing lesson plans, but too many don't take you anywhere. *Objectives should rule. Programs should serve.* A program is good if it helps you take another step toward your objective. A program is bad if it does not move you along.

Let me illustrate this concept.

Let's go back to my college illustration of a few paragraphs ago. You probably know that every college or university has a student recruitment program. Some are good so they continue to be used every year, with about the same results. Others are innovative and have remarkable results.

My small college faced the fact that we needed more students. We had a faculty and ample facilities to serve many more students then we generally had. Our objective was to get our student enrollment up.

We were convinced that if the thousands of high school seniors knew more about our college, we would have many more students. We pondered out objective over many months and came up with a new program of student recruitment. We named the program "Get Acquainted With *XYZ College*."

The basic idea was to offer high school seniors a summer trip to London in order to get acquainted with the college. First, we approached the airlines to see what it would cost to charter a plane or two to take the students to

London. The bids came in and the cost per student was low. Next we approached some hotels in London to see what it would cost to house all of the students for one week. The bids came back. The costs were low. We could afford it.

Then a small group of faculty developed daily programs for the students while they were in England. Buses were hired. Guides were secured. It was a real dream trip for the students, and the cost was low enough that the trip could be given to the students as a graduation present—parents, uncles and aunts, friends all participated in the program.

We purchased a mailing list of 100,000 graduating seniors in our State. We sent them brochures about the trip and the activities planned for each day of the trip. The response was overwhelming. In the end we took several hundred seniors to London for a week. Nightly we had programs designed for entertainment and recruitment. The fears that many had about the program were erased. The trip paid for itself.

And, the resultant enrollment that fall term was the largest in the school's history. The program had helped the college reach its objective. It was a good program. The secret was in good prior planning.

Step Three
What Kind, and How Many Persons Will The Program Require?

The nature of any venture will require staffing—people to perform each phase of the venture. Developing a program is difficult, and getting personnel to carry out a program is more difficult. More ventures fail at the people step, than at any *concept* step.

Many great efforts have failed simply because the venture was not able to find the right people to staff it. On the other hand the success of many other ventures have come about because there was a cadre of volunteers who were willing to participate.

In America, more than in any other country, there seems to be large numbers of volunteers who will be willing to contribute their labor or expertise to a worthy project.

That speaks well for our nation. But, there is a growing trend toward inertia, because ventures do not have enough money to carry them through. Reliance on money is a great handicap. Generosity of time and talent is a resource large enough to give success to nearly any venture.

I am convinced that where there is a need, there is a willingness among people in the community to fulfill it. The success in America has not been because of its wealth; it has been because the people are willing to do whatever they are called on to do. America is composed of *givers*—not *takers*.

Step Four
What Tools and Space Does The Program Require?

Today, as in no other time, we have **more** tools to help us do any thing that needs to be done, than we have ever had before. In addition, we have **better** tools than at any time in history. The computer is the "mother of miracles," and almost anyone today owns at least one and is trained in its use.

In our time no great project will ever be conceived or completed without the use of a computer. And, there is always someone around who can make it dance.

The availability of graphics, design, and communications is so advanced that the possibilities are almost without boundaries. We are surrounded with amazing hardware and software. Today, **what the mind can conceive and** believe is not a cliche. Our tools and training have made that phrase—**reality**.

In this present slice of time, private individuals are dreaming about going to the moon, and they have activated plans to make it possible. Already, private citizens have made their reservations.

(Give me moment of fantasy, please.)

I can see an announcement in your church's bulletin. "Don't forget to make your reservation for next Saturday's church picnic. The picnic will be held on the moon. The church's rocket will leave promptly at 7:00 a.m. and will arrive back by 7:00 in the evening.

"See Deacon Jones and pay your $100 fee, and that will include a meal and a snack. There will also be refreshments on the rocket for your trip home.

"You will also be interested in knowing that we are already planning our Spring picnic. We plan to take a full weekend since we will be going to Mars. I hear that the view of earth from Mars is spectacular.

"Pastor Smith has already bought a new pair of binoculars. He plans to find Heaven and look at it. He wants to see Saint Peter standing at the Golden Gates. Don't be late."

(The fantasy is over. Let's get back to reality.)

It is probably not necessary to say this, but I will. Do not forget to make one person responsible for all tools and equipment. If more than one person is assigned to that task, you most certainly will lose things, or forget to get them. Each task should be assigned a definite responsibility, and all participants in the project should know who that person is.

An itinerary should be made and each person with an assignment should have a copy of it. The schedule of activities should be known by everyone.

**Step Five
How Will You Move
Your Project Forward?**

Programs are mostly inert and they will stay that way until some spark ignites them—or they are prodded to move along—or they are propelled into action by some internal or external *force*. Programs are typically lazy. They will lie there in all of their beauty, until they are forced to move on.

Take government for example. Hundreds of elected officials work long and hard to develop programs designed to help citizens. Finally, an agreement is reached and a program is passed on to the President for signature.

Ultimately, the President signs the work of congress and then it is passes on to the bureaucrats for implementation. Often—too often—that is the last time it is heard of. Bureaucrats "fine tune" the new program and pass it on from one committee to another for their input of regulations to control the program. Somewhere along the line the program goes to sleep— like Rip Van Winkle.

The programs developed by a single individual or a small group are not immune to those processes that impede governmental action. I confess that many of my own ideas and programs have never been enacted. They rest—dust covered in the attic of my brain— and its sad that they will never be awakened and stirred to action. (I have also created an encyclopedia of excuses why they sleep on—year after year). Many of us have missed the seminar on How To Get Things Done— **GTD**.

Before any money is spent on a program—before any announcement is made—a clear vision of **Program Promotion** must be developed and adopted by all of the leaders of the project.

Many developers of a particular project will find that this **Step Five** will be a great place for a *detour*. They will erect a large sign saying **"This road is under construction and will be opened shortly." Shortly**, scarcely ever comes. Program benefits will die and even the most vivid of dreams will never see the light of day. ……**R.I.P.**

Step Six
How Will We Organize All Of The Above?

The **organization** of the parts and people within a single enterprise is of utmost importance. If too little thought is given to the way things and processes are structured will leave the participants and prospects in confusion

For illustration and clarity let's say that the effort in a particular case is to create and contribute a scholarship to a bright young orphan in the community. In the endeavor we have already considered the first five steps of getting something done, and we have come to Step Six—organizaation.

How will we organize the venture? It could be constructed in a number of ways: as a corporation, company, foundation, association, partnership, fellowship, non-profit organization, or just as a group of friends, a fellowship or program.

Thus far we have focused on the internal organization of the effort. In addition there is always an external system of connections. Often these external connections can be more important than the internal structures.

The leader should ask himself:

- How do we relate to the economic forces at work in the community?
- Should we reach out to the local charitable foundations?
- Are there prominent members in the community who are generous with financial assistance?
- How can we get individuals of reputation to endorse the project?
- Perhaps an advisory board can be developed to provide substance to the project.
- How can we connect to local politicians and community leaders to support our cause?
- How can we connect with the media to promote our causer?

These are only a few things that should be considered in relation to organizing to reach a final goal or objective. The head of the venture is the one most responsible for making sure that Step Six has been fully considered.

Step Seven
What Budget Must We Have To Pay For The Above Steps?

Nearly every step in the process of GTD has economic implications. Someone in the venture should be appointed to guide the effort in auditing the financial needs of each step. There is no need to outline the obvious attributes of such a business manager.

On the other hand the venture may not involve numerous people, but be a project of a single person. It nevertheless must have consideration of all of the implications of finance.

This is just another way of saying that someone must count the cost of the plan. Nothing of real importance can be done without someone paying for the processes of the venture.

Many dreams die at this step. Sloppy financial planning is the cause for mosts failures and few are helped by failure. Many are hurt by it.

Don't bury your dreams in the cemetery of remorse.

Step Eight
How Do The Above
Look On A Calendar?

Don't forget the calendar. Everything that happens, happens on some date. In the course of planning to reach a goal or objective the calendar comes into play. There are certain events that will happen and they will impact the calendar.

Seeing each element of the plan scheduled for a specific date helps the planner. For instance in planning for an event one will look at the calendar and see if it is available. Even scheduling an event around Christmas, thanksgiving, Easter, graduation, etc. can be a difficult task. That is why all 10 Steps should be placed on paper and then transferred to a calendar.

Another consideration is that everyone has a calendar. All leaders. in the venture already have firm dates on their calendars. So, the venture calendar must be checked against the calendars of all important leaders of the venture. Doing so will give efficiency to the project and will protect against scheduling conflicts.

Step Nine

What Indices Will We Use To Evaluate The Above?

Yardsticks and rulers are important and necessary for gauging progress. About anything has to have a way of evaluating whether the position points to success.

If person has the goal of going to New York, City and he leaves from Fargo North Dakota, he has to have some way of evaluating his progress toward his goal. After one day of travel he finds that he is in Denver, he certainly must re-think his goal. After two days of travel he is in Reno, Nevada. He has to pause and either abandon his goal or make some serious adjustments.

If a person sets out to raise a million dollars for a scholarship fund and after a couple of months he has raised only $17.00 he must re-examine his goal, his method of fund-raising, or the quality of personnel assigned to raise the money.

In any venture some index must be established to guide those who lead. Ignoring progress endangers the dream.

Step Ten
Is Our Objective Worth The Effort?

One good thing about having a 10 Step plan for reaching an objective is that the process will alert the promoters at several stages as to whether the work is worth the effort and cost or not. Large ventures or small ventures should not be immune to periodic evaluation.

"Drain the swamp" is a lofty and noble goal but the 10 Step methodology is inclined to discouragement during the period of planning—let alone during the period of action. It is indeed amazing that anything can ever be accomplished, but it happens and it needs a framework.

Enthusiasm for the objective is high at the beginning but more often than not it drops when effort is required. Someone should always be there to shout "Git her done."

Summary of the 10 Steps

1. What is/are my OBJECTIVES?
   (short term — long term)

2. What PROGRAMS will be necessary?

3. How many and what kinds of PERSONNEL will these PROGRAMS require?

4. How should I ORGANIZE this PERSONNEL and these PROGRAMS?

5. What SPACE and TOOLS will be required?

6. How will I PROMOTE
   (give motion) to these entities?

7. What will be the necessary costs (BUDGET) for the above?

8. How will the above fit on a CALENDAR?

9. What indices will I use to EVALUATE the above effort and cost?

10. Are the goals worth the effort?

Companion Books in the Win With Wisdom Series

"WISE Methods for WISE people"
Take Ten Steps to Reach Your Goals

Nearly everyone knows WHAT the goals are or WHAT they want. Few people know HOW to get the WHAT. A new movement has been formed to help people capture the skill of HOW to get things done, or as they call it how to **GTD**.

This book is a primer or beginners guide. It is a road map which anyone can read or follow. It involves moving from a beginning point to a second point and then through eight other points which will help nearly anyone to GTD or arrive at a desirable destination.

Any reader who will invest less than an hour of their time(and $6) will be rewarded with a tool worth thousands of dollars and hours of new time.

"Save Yourselves with WISDOM"
How to Avoid the Dangers of Tomorrow

Tomorrow will bring a cup of promise and a vat of dangers. No one will be exempt from either. The only solution is to get to know both, and plan to avoid the dangers and profit from the promises.

Central to the book is a letter written by a wealthy tycoon to his wealthy clients. What he writes is appropriate for the rich and important for average families as well. To ignore his warnings would be sheer folly.

This book faces the warnings head-on and points to practical solutions. An investment of only minutes of your time could be the best investment that you will make this year. The letter is a must-read.

"It's WISE To Know The Big Picture"
The strategies of Getting by Giving

This book is based on a story told by a very wealthy investor to an educator seeking a large financial gift. The educator received NO MONEY, but he was given a valuable secret that would always bring wealth to anyone brave enough to use it.

The book is small and is on sale for only $6.00 and a few minutes of your time, but you and the ones that you care about should have it. It could change your future.

"The WISDOM of Knowing yourself and others."
Why you and others do what you do

Psychology has become one of the most popular studies in colleges and universities. Unfortunately it has been seized by the academicians who have morphed it into a complex tool, available only to the esoteric.

This book molds psychology into a useful everyday tool for average persons. There are no long words or complex formulas. The average person can use what he reads to understand himself and those with whom he lives and works.

That it is a commonsense book for daily living is its merit. Don't show it to your professor, analyst or therapist. Read it yourself and use it daily.

"WISDOM on Fire"
It takes more than one stick to burn BIG

This small book is big on emotion, concepts and inspiration. It can be read in less than an hour, but it should be read only a few pages at a time.

And even if your memory is fading you will remember many phrases, sentences and passages for years to come. This book will be a unique experience. And it is only $6 on sale from the author. Amazon prices it only two dollars more. Don't miss it.

These books are all available from Amazon.com. Go to Amazon, and on Amazons search type in: Kenneth Shelby Armstrong Books. Select the book that you want and pay Amazon.

In addition to the books in the Win With Wisdom are several longer books written buy Dr. Armstrong. In all of the six books listed below you will find phrases of wisdom and humor. If you have difficulty in finding the books, just call Dr. Armstrong and he will help

To contact the author.
Author: Kenneth Shelby Armstrong Th.D., Ed.D.
Email: KennethWrites@me.com
Phone: 1-580-873-2377
Address: 1036 Holiday Acres Drive
              Fort Towson, OK 74735

Whatever Happened To Robin?

Kenneth Shelby Armstrong
Publisher: Create Space
Available: Amazon or
Direct from Author
347 Pages
Copyright 2015

On the shores of Lake Biwa near Kyoto, Japan, a distinguished American bishop laid his head in the lap of a lovely Japanese woman and died. His death opened a secret that he had held since he was a young G.I. exploring the ruins of Hiroshima and Nagasaki with a young Japanese girl friend. The explosion of the secret shook a prominent American family and its church.

When he left Japan he promised to return and marry the girl of his dreams, but circumstances caused him to break that promise. Nevertheless, each New Year's Day he wrote her letters reaffirming his love and promising to return to her.

For decades he served his church as Bishop, but he never gave up his pledge to return to Robin. Nearing death he could delay no longer so he, used what strength he had to return to Japan and he laid his head in the lap of a lovely woman and died. But, to know the real secret you must read Whatever Happened to Robin?.

Will It Be Dangerous? Could I Get Killed?

Kenneth Shelby Armstrong
Publisher: Create Space
Available: Amazon or Direct from Author
129 Pages
Copyright 2015

"No! No! No! You're looking at this thing all wrong. This will be a great educational experience. Just think of it! It's 1953 and segregation is the law of the State of Georgia and most other States in the South. A white graduate student walks into an all-negro University, say Atlanta University, and tries to enroll. What do you think would happen? This could be a life-changing experience for you, and it could bring about real change."

"That's what I'm thinking about. This life-changing experiment could get me killed. Have you ever heard of the Ku Klux Klan? If they hear about this I will be dead meat. If by some miracle the university should let me in, they will be breaking the law. It's illegal for them to accept a white student. I could even go to jail. I could get killed. And what if your Dean heard that you were advising one of your students to break the law? It could get you fired. But why should I worry? I'll be dead." The story of the book is, that I did get enrolled and I'm still alive and significantly more educated.

How To Strive, Thrive, And Stay Alive in Prison

Kenneth Shelby Armstrong
Publisher: Create Space
Available: Amazon or
Direct from Author
117 Pages
Copyright 2015

More than a million prisoners are now behind bars; eating three bland meals a day with never a change; each night they are serenaded by a chorus of snores from which there is no escape; they spend time in planning revenge on some member of their families or some policeman or judge who did them wrong; they wait for that special letter that never comes. Too often mail call is a downer. It's a tough life for the men, but much harder on the women.

Broken dreams become nightmares. Soft memories are crushed by harsh treatment from detention officials. Visiting hours are too brief and saying goodbye to family and small children erupts in tears that will continue for hours.

But some in prison find forgiveness and others discover that there is hope. Some discover beauty in unexpected places. Faith, hope, and love, live there too.

My Very Best Stories

Kenneth Shelby Armstrong
Publisher: Create Space
Available: Amazon or
Direct from Author
138 Pages
Copyright 2015

    There is a really great editor/owner of the newspaper in the town where I live. He knows everybody and everybody knows him. In these days there are few towns and newspapers like the one we have in Hugo, Oklahoma. I read his editorials every day and hidden inside of each one is pungent information, sparkling humor, and honest concern for the town where he has lived all of his life, and which many of us have adopted.

    Against all odds he has kept our newspaper something that we look forward to getting. One day he asked me to let him publish some of my short stories in the paper. I gladly accepted the assignment. It was so well received that we decided to publish those stories in a book. It's now available and the range of interest is broad enough to capture the interest of people even though they live in New York City or Los Angeles. These are stories for everyone.

I Was A Reluctant Guest

Kenneth Shelby Armstrong
Publisher: Create Space
Available: Amazon or
Direct from Author
236 Pages
Copyright 2015

    Being in prison can be an exciting adventure. Every inmate has some great story to tell–and that over and over again. But the stories that come from prison are rooted in a minutia of facts, most of which are boring and void of meaning. The facts of each prisoner's case may be interesting only to a weird attorney or some other prisoner who is looking for some way to get out. What do you do when you are looking at twenty years in each dreadful place?

    Of more interest than facts are the emotions and feelings alive in each prison. For the most part the emotions are kept within specifically prescribed boundaries, but too often they spill out like volcanic ash. The results can be fights, riots, and escapes. Neither guards nor reluctant guests look forward to such events. But you will begin to understand the drama of prison, inside and out.

He Died A Hero

Kenneth Shelby Armstrong
Publisher: Create Space
Available: Amazon or
Direct from Author
211 Pages
Copyright 2015

In our current culture a hero is someone, dressed in a cape and flying through the air with the greatest of ease to release some damsel who has gotten into the clutches of an ogre with warts. Of course the drama takes place on some remote planet located just above Kansas City. The plot is compelling and people will pay $15 just to experience the unreality of some weirdo's imagination.

On the other hand an unadorned reality is a country boy wearing patched overalls and sporting a straw hat with holes in the brim and a black sweat band earned while picking cotton under an Oklahoma sun, to earn a few cents to put bread on the table during the peak of the Great Depression. After supper he will study until his eye lids shut his brain down, but he is committed to getting a college education–the first in his family. With the diploma placed in the back pocket of his overalls he marched out to serve his God and those in need. What a Story!

These books are all available from Amazon.com.
Go to Amazon, and on Amazons search type in:
Kenneth Shelby Armstrong Books. Select the book that you want and pay Amazon.
======================================

To contact the author.

Author: Kenneth Shelby Armstrong Th.D., Ed.D.

Email: KennethWrites@me.com

Phone: 1-580-873-2377

Address: 1036 Holiday Acres Drive
            Fort Towson, OK 74735

www.ingramcontent.com/pod-product-compliance
Lightning Source LLC
Chambersburg PA
CBHW061227180526
45170CB00003B/1194